W9-BWU-976

Chunky Cabled Hat

Yarn (5)

- 260yd/238m, 7oz/200g of any bulky weight acrylic/wool/nylon yarn in yellow

Needles

- One pair size 10 (6mm) needles
  or size to obtain gauge

Notions

- Cable needle (cn)

■■■□□ □

Size

Sized for Adult Woman.

Measurements

- **Head circumference** 15"/38cm
- **Length** 9¼"/23.5cm

Note Hat will stretch to fit.

Gauge

21 sts and 24 rows to 4"/10cm over double cable pat using size 10 (6mm) needles. *Take time to check gauge.*

Pom Pom

1 Following the template on page 16, cut two circular pieces of cardboard.

2 Hold the two circles together and wrap the yarn tightly around the cardboard. Carefully cut around the cardboard.

3 Tie a piece of yarn tightly between the two circles. Remove the cardboard and trim the pom pom.

Stitch Glossary

6-st LC Sl 3 sts to cn and hold to *front*, k3, k3 from cn.

6-st RC Sl 3 sts to cn and hold to *back*, k3, k3 from cn.

K1, P1 Rib

(over an odd number of sts)

Row 1 (RS) K1, *p1, k1; rep from * to end.

Row 2 (WS) K the knit sts and p the purl sts. Rep row 2 for k1, p1 rib.

Double Cable Pattern

(multiple of 11 sts plus 2)

Rows 1, 3, 9 and 11 (RS) *P2, k9; rep from * to last 2 sts, p2.

Row 2 and all WS rows K2, *p9, k2; rep from * to end.

Row 5 *P2, 6-st LC, k3; rep from * to last 2 sts, p2.

Row 7 *P2, k3, 6-st RC; rep from * to last 2 sts, p2.

Row 12 Rep row 2.

Rep rows 1–12 for double cable pat.

Hat

Cast on 79 sts. Work in k1, p1 rib for 2½"/6.5cm.

Beg double cable pat

Work rows 1–12 of double cable pat until piece measures 7½"/19cm from beg, end with a WS row.

Shape crown

Next (dec) row (RS) *K3, k2tog; rep from * to last 4 sts, k4—64 sts.

Purl 1 row, knit 1 row, purl 1 row.

Next (dec) row (RS) *K1, k2tog; rep from * to last 4 sts, k4—44 sts.

Purl 1 row, knit 1 row.

Next (dec) row (WS) *P1, p2tog; rep from * to last 2 sts, p2—30 sts.

Next row Knit.

Next (dec) row (WS) *P2tog; rep from * to end—15 sts.

Cut yarn, leaving a long tail. Thread yarn through rem sts and pull tight to close. Sew back seam.

Finishing

Make a 4"/10cm pom pom and secure to top of hat. ■

tip

Always use more yarn than you think you need for your pom pom. Trim it down until it feels like velvet!

Houndstooth Hat

Yarn ④
- 99yd/90m, 1¾oz/50g of any worsted weight wool/acrylic yarn in blue (A), gray (B), and red (C)

Needles
- One each sizes 7 and 8 (4.5 and 5mm) circular needles, 16"/40 long *or size to obtain gauge*
- One set (4) size 8 (5mm) double-pointed needles (dpns)

Notions
- Stitch marker

Size
Sized for Adult Woman.

Measurements
- **Brim circumference** 18"/45.5cm
- **Length** 11"/28cm

Gauge
21 sts and 19 rnds to 4"/10cm over St st using larger needle.
Take time to check gauge.

Pom Pom
1 Following the template on page 16, cut two circular pieces of cardboard.
2 Hold the two circles together and wrap the yarn tightly around the cardboard. Carefully cut around the cardboard.
3 Tie a piece of yarn tightly between the two circles. Remove the cardboard and trim the pom pom.

Hat
With A and smaller needle, cast on 104 sts. Join, taking care not to twist sts, and place marker for beg of rnd.

Rnd 1 *With A, k2, with C, k2; rep from * around.
Rnd 2 *With A, k2, with C, p2; rep from * around.
Rep rnd 2 for corrugated rib for 8 rnds more. Cut C. Change to larger needle.

Beg chart 1
Rnd 1 Work 4-st rep 26 times around. Cont to work chart 1 in this way through rnd 4, then rep rnds 1–4 until piece measures 8½"/21.5cm from beg, end with a rnd 4.

Beg chart 2
Note Change to dpns when sts no longer fit comfortably on circular needle.
Rnd 1 Work rnd 1 for 13 times around. Cont to work chart 2 in this way through rnd 13—13 sts.
Cut yarn and thread through rem sts. Pull tightly and secure.
With C, make a 2"/5cm pom pom and secure to top of hat. ■

CHART 1
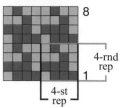

4-rnd rep
4-st rep
8
1

CHART 2
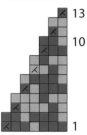

13
10
1

COLOR KEY
■ blue (A)
■ gray (B)

STITCH KEY
□ k on RS
☒ k2tog

tip
When carrying two colors across the back of your hat, be sure not to pull too tightly!

Welted Hat

Yarn

- 95yd/87m, 1¾oz/50g of any worsted weight wool in blue (MC) and green (CC)

Needles

- One size 7 (4.5mm) circular needle, 16"/40cm long *or size to obtain gauge*
- One size 5 (3.75mm) circular needle, 16"/40cm long
- One set (5) size 7 (4.5mm) double-pointed needles (dpns)

Notions

- Stitch marker

Size

Sized for Adult Woman.

Measurements

- **Brim circumference** (unstretched) 16"/40.5cm
- **Length** (unstretched) 6½"/16.5cm

Gauge

19 sts and 24 rnds to 4"/10cm over St st using larger needles.
Take time to check gauge.

K1, P1 Twisted Rib

(over an even number of sts)
Rnd 1 (RS) *K1 tbl, p1; rep from * to end.
Rep rnd 1 for k1, p1 twisted rib.

Cap

With MC and smaller needle, cast on 90 sts. Place marker for beg of rnd and join, taking care not to twist sts.
Work in k1, p1 twisted rib for 6 rnds.
Next (inc) rnd [K9, M1] 10 times—100 sts.

Beg welted stripe

Change to larger needle.
Rnd 1 With CC, knit.
Rnds 2–6 With CC, purl.
Rnds 7–10 With MC, knit.
Rep rnds 1–10 three times more, then work rnds 1–6 once more.
Cut CC and work in MC only to end.

Shape crown

Note Change to dpns when there are too few sts to fit comfortably on circular needle.
Next (dec) rnd [K8, k2tog] 10 times—90 sts.
K 1 rnd.
Next (dec) rnd [K7, k2tog] 10 times—80 sts.
K 1 rnd.
Next (dec) rnd [K6, k2tog] 10 times—70 sts.
K 1 rnd.
Next (dec) rnd [K5, k2tog] 10 times—60 sts.
K 1 rnd.
Next (dec) rnd [K4, k2tog] 10 times—50 sts.
K 1 rnd.
Next (dec) rnd [K3, k2tog] 10 times—40 sts.
K 1 rnd.
Next (dec) rnd [K2, k2tog] 10 times—30 sts.
K 1 rnd.
Next (dec) rnd [K1, k2tog] 10 times—20 sts.
K 1 rnd.
Next (dec) rnd [K2tog] 10 times—10 sts.
K 1 rnd.
Cut yarn, leaving a long tail. Thread yarn through rem sts and pull tight to close. ■

Tassled Hat

Yarn 4
- 200yd/182m, 7oz/200g of any worsted weight wool yarn in pink

Needles
- One pair size 9 (5.5mm) needles *or size to obtain gauge*

Notions
- Removable stitch markers

Measurements
- **Length** (from top to lower edge) 10"/25.5cm
- **Width** (from brim to back tassel) 11"/28cm

Gauge
17 sts and 26 rows to 4"/10cm over St st using size 9 (5.5mm) needles after blocking. *Take time to check gauge.*

Knit/Purl Stripe Pattern
Rows 1, 3 and 5 (RS) Purl.
Rows 2, 4 and 6 (WS) Knit.
Rows 7, 9 and 11 (RS) Knit.
Rows 8, 10 and 12 (WS) Purl.
Rep rows 1–12 for knit/purl stripe pat.

Hat
Cast on 92 sts. Work rows 1–12 of knit/purl stripe pat twice, placing marker at end of last row. Do not slip this marker. Cont in pat, work as foll:
Next (dec) row (RS) P2, ssp, p to last 4 sts, p2tog, p2—2 sts dec'd.
Rep dec row every other row twice more—86 sts. Work one row even.
Next (dec) row (RS) K2, ssk, k to last 4 sts, k2tog, k2.
Rep dec row every other row twice more—80 sts. Work one row even.

Beg garter st cap
Next row (RS) K2, ssk, k to last 4 sts, k2tog, k2.
Next row (WS) Knit.
Rep last 2 rows 11 times more—56 sts. Pm in fabric after 28th st of last row. Bind off.

Brim
With RS facing, pick up and k 92 sts along cast-on edge (one for every st).
Row 1 (WS) P4, *k4, p4; rep from * to end.
Row 2 (RS) K4, *p4, k4; rep from * to end.
Rep last 2 rows until brim measures 3"/7.5cm, end with a WS row. Bind off in pat.

Finishing
Block lightly. Fold hat in half. Sew tog between markers.

Tassel (make 3)
Wrap yarn approx 20 times around a piece of cardboard 3"/7.5cm long. Thread a strand of yarn, insert it in the cardboard and tie it at the top, leaving a long end to tie around the tassel. Cut the lower edge to free the strands. Wrap the long tail tightly several times around the upper edge and insert the ends into the tassel. Trim the strands. Attach one tassel to each corner of brim and one to top back. ■

Diagonal Stitch Hat

Yarn ④
- 218yd/200m, 3½oz/100g of any worsted weight wool yarn in self-striping design

Needles
- One size 7 (4.5mm) circular needle, 16"/40cm long *or size to obtain gauge*
- One set (5) size 7 (4.5mm) double-pointed needles (dpns)

Notions
- Stitch markers

Size
Sized for Adult Woman, slouchy style (beanie style).

Measurements
- **Head circumference** 20½ (16½)"/52 (42)cm
- **Length** 11 (7¼)"/28 (18.5)cm

Gauge
16 sts and 30 rows to 4"/10cm over garter st using size 7 (4.5mm) needles.
Take time to check gauge.

K1, P1 Rib
(over an even number of sts)
Rnd 1 (RS) *K1, p1; rep from * around.
Rep rnd 1 for k1, p1 rib.

Notes
1 Body of hat is worked flat, then seamed.
2 Ribbed brim and crown are formed by picking up sts along edges after body is complete.
3 Place marker to indicate RS when working garter st body.

Hat
Cast on 3 sts.
Row 1 (inc RS) Kfb, kfb, k1—5 sts.
Row 2 (WS) Knit.
Row 3 (inc RS) Kfb, k to last 2 sts, kfb, k1—2 sts inc'd. Rep rows 2 and 3 until piece measures 8½ (4¾")/21.5 (12)cm from beg, measured along side edge (end of RS rows), end with a RS row.
Next row (WS) Knit.
Next row (RS) Kfb, k to last 3 sts, k2tog, k1. Rep last 2 rows until long edge of piece (beg of RS rows) measures 20½ (16½)"/52 (42)cm from beg, end with a RS row.
Next row (WS) Knit.
Next row (dec RS) K1, ssk, k to last 3 sts, k2tog, k1—2 sts dec'd.
Rep last 2 rows until 5 sts rem.
Next row (WS) Knit.
Next row (RS) Ssk, k1, k2tog—3 sts. Bind off. Block piece to rectangle shape. Sew shorter edges tog to form a tube.

Brim
With circular needle, pick up and k 88 sts around either open edge of tube. Place marker for beg of rnd and join, taking care not to twist sts. Work in k1, p1 rib for 5 rnds. Bind off in rib.

Shape crown
Note Change to dpns when there are too few sts to fit comfortably on circular needle. With circular needle, pick up and k 65 sts around opposite open edge of tube. Place marker for beg of rnd and join, taking care not to twist sts.
Rnd 1 Knit.
Rnd 2 *P2tog, p3; rep from * around—52 sts.
Rnd 3 Knit.
Rnd 4 P2, *p2tog, p3; rep from * around—42 sts.
Rnd 5 Knit.
Rnd 6 P2, *p2tog, p2; rep from * around—32 sts.
Rnd 7 Knit.
Rnd 8 *P2tog; rep from * around—16 sts.
Rnd 9 *K2tog; rep from * around—8 sts.
Cut yarn, leaving a long tail. Thread yarn through rem sts and pull tight to close. ∎

style tip
While this hat looks great in a self-striping yarn, it would also be wonderful in a solid color, or with a contrasting brim.

Striped Hat

Yarn
- 200yd/183m, 2oz/55g of any DK weight wool in pink (A) and blue (B)

Needles
- One size 6 (4mm) circular needle, 16"/40cm long *or size to obtain gauge*
- One set (5) size 6 (4mm) double-pointed needles (dpns)

Notions
- Stitch marker
- Tapestry needle

Size
Sized for Adult Woman.

Measurements
- **Circumference** (around ribbed brim) 17"/43cm
- **Length** 11"/28cm

Gauge
25 sts and 36 rnds to 4"/10cm over St st using size 6 (4mm) needles.
Take time to check gauge.

Hat
With circular needle and A, cast on 108 sts, place marker (pm) and join, being careful not to twist. Work in k2, p2 rib until piece measures 2"/5cm from beg. Cont with A, work in St st (k every rnd) until piece measures 4¼"/11cm from beg. Cont in St st, with B work for 2½"/6.5cm. With A, work for 2½"/6.5cm. With B work until piece measures 9¾"/24.5cm from beg.

Shape crown
Note Change to dpns when sts no longer comfortably fit on circular needle.
Cont in St st with B and beg to shape crown as foll:

Next (dec) rnd *K7, k2tog; rep from * to end—96 sts. Knit 1 rnd.
Next (dec) rnd *K6, k2tog; rep from * around—84 sts. Knit 1 rnd.
Next (dec) rnd *K5, k2tog; rep from * around—72 sts. Knit 1 rnd.
Next (dec) rnd *K4, k2tog; rep from * around—60 sts. Cont to dec every rnd, working 1 less st before each k2tog until 24 sts rem.
Next (dec) rnd *K2tog; rep from * around—12 sts. Cut yarn, leaving long tail, and thread through rem sts.

Finishing
With tapestry needle and 36"/91.5cm length of A, beg on WS just above rib, sew running st up one column of sts to crown, turn and sew running st down next column of sts, to beg of rib. Pull tails to gather to desired shape. Tie off. ■

Tassle-Tied Cap

Yarn
- 275yd/251m, 3½oz/100g of any DK weight wool/cotton yarn in multi

Needles
- One each sizes 3 and 6 (3.25 and 4mm) circular needles, 16"/40cm long *or size to obtain gauge*

Notions
- Stitch marker

Size
Sized for Adult Woman.

Measurements
- **Circumference at wide edge untied** 20"/51cm
- **Length** 12"/30.5cm

Gauge
22 sts and 28 rows to 4"/10cm over St st using larger needles.
Take time to check gauge.

Stitch Glossary
RT K 2nd st on LH needle, do not drop from needle, k first st and drop both sts from LH needle.

Hat
With smaller needle, cast on 112 sts. Join, taking care not to twist the sts, and place marker for beg of rnd.
Rnds 1 and 2 *K2, p2; rep from * around.
Rnd 3 *RT, p2; rep from * around. Rep rnds 1–3 for twist rib pat 8 times more, then rep rnds 1–2 once more.
Next (inc) rnd [K14, M1] 8 times around—120 sts. Change to larger needle. Work even in St st (k every rnd) until piece measures 11"/28cm from beg.

Next (dec) rnd [K13, k2tog] 8 times—112 sts. K 2 rnds. Change to smaller needle.
Next (eyelet) rnd *K3, yo, k2tog; rep from * to last 2 sts, k2. Rep twist rib rnds 1–3 twice, then rep rnds 1 and 2 once more. Bind off loosely in rib.

Finishing
Cut four 108"/274cm lengths of yarn. Make a twisted cord by knotting ends together and twisting tightly, allowing cord to twist back on itself. String cord through eyelets.

Tassels (make 2)
Wrap yarn approx 50 times around a piece of cardboard 3"/7.5cm long. Thread a strand of yarn, insert it in the cardboard and tie it at the top, leaving a long end to tie around the tassel. Cut the lower edge to free the strands. Wrap the long tail tightly several times around the upper edge and insert the ends into the tassel. Trim the strands. Secure one tassel to each end of cord. ■

Textured Watch Cap

Yarn [4]
- 220yd/201m, 3½oz/100g of any worsted weight wool in teal

Needles
- One size 6 (4mm) circular needle, 16"/40cm long *or size to obtain gauge*
- One set (5) size 6 (4mm) double-pointed needles (dpns)

Notions
- Stitch marker

Size
Sized for Adult Woman.

Measurements
- **Head circumference** 20"/51cm
- **Length** (with folded brim) 8¼"/21cm

Gauge
20 sts and 30 rnds to 4"/10cm over lozenge pat using size 6 (4mm) needles. *Take time to check gauge.*

Lozenge Pattern
(multiple of 5 sts)

Rnd 1 *P4, k1; rep from * around.
Rnd 2 *P3, k2; rep from * around.
Rnd 3 *P2, k3; rep from * around.
Rnd 4 *P1, k4; rep from * around.
Rnd 5 *K1, p4; rep from * around.
Rnd 6 *K2, p3; rep from * around.
Rnd 7 *K3, p2; rep from * around.
Rnd 8 *K4, p1; rep from * around.
Rep rnds 1–8 for lozenge pat.

Pom Pom
1 Following the template on page 16, cut two circular pieces of cardboard.

2 Hold the two circles together and wrap the yarn tightly around the cardboard. Carefully cut around the cardboard.

3 Tie a piece of yarn tightly between the two circles. Remove cardboard and trim pom pom.

Hat
With circular needle, cast on 100 sts. Place marker for beg of rnd and join, taking care not to twist sts. Work in lozenge pat until piece measures 9"/23cm, end with a row 4.

Shape crown
Note Change to dpns when there are too few sts to fit comfortably on circular needle.
Rnd 1 (dec) [K1, p2tog, p2, k1, p4] 10 times—90 sts.
Rnd 2 [K2, p2, k2, p3] 10 times.
Rnd 3 (dec) [K2, p2tog, k3, p2] 10 times—80 sts.
Rnd 4 [K7, p1] 10 times.
Rnd 5 (dec) [P1, k2tog, p4, k1] 10 times—70 sts.
Rnd 6 [P5, k2] 10 times.
Rnd 7 (dec) [P2tog, p2, k3] 10 times—60 sts.
Rnd 8 (dec) [P2tog, k4] 10 times—50 sts.
Rnd 9 [K1, p4] 10 times.
Rnd 10 (dec) [K2, p2tog, p1] 10 times—40 sts.
Rnd 11 [K3, p1] 10 times.
Rnd 12 (dec) [K2, k2tog] 10 times—30 sts.
Rnd 13 Knit.
Rnd 14 (dec) [K2tog] 15 times—15 sts.
Cut yarn, leaving a long tail. Thread yarn through rem sts and pull tight to close.

Finishing
Make a 4"/10cm pom pom and secure to top of hat. Fold brim approx 2"/5cm to RS. ■

extra
Try this hat with a slightly heavier yarn for the man in your life. You can leave the pom pom off if that's more his style.

Cabled & Embroidered Hat

Yarn 4
- 75yd/68m, 1¾oz/50g of any worsted weight cotton yarn in purple (MC) and orange (CC)

Needles
- One size 7 (4.5mm) circular needle, 16"/40cm long *or size to obtain gauge*
- One set (5) size 7 (4.5mm) double-pointed needles (dpns)

Notions
- Stitch arker
- Cable needle (cn)
- Tapestry needle

Sizes
Sized for Adult Woman.

Measurements
- **Head circumference** 19"/48.5cm
- **Length** 8½"/21.5cm

Gauge
30 sts and 31 rnds to 4"/10cm over cable pat using size 7 (4.5mm) needles.
Take time to check gauge.

Pom Pom
1 Following the template on page 16, cut two circular pieces of cardboard.
2 Hold the two circles together and wrap the yarn tightly around the cardboard. Carefully cut around the cardboard.
3 Tie a piece of yarn tightly between the two circles. Remove cardboard and trim pom pom.

Stitch Glossary
6-st LC Sl 3 sts to cn and hold to *front*, k3, k3 from cn.

K2, P2 Rib
(multiple of 4 sts)
Rnd 1 *K2, p2; rep from * around.
Rep rnd 1 for k2, p2 rib.

Hat
With MC and circular needle, cast on 108 sts. Place marker for beg of rnd and join, taking care not to twist sts. Work in k2, p2 rib for 7 rnds.
Next (inc) rnd *K3, M1; rep from * around—144 sts.

Beg cable pat
Rnds 1–7 *K6, p3; rep from * around.
Rnd 8 *6-st LC, p3; rep from * around.
Rep rnds 1–8 until piece measures 7¼"/18.5cm from beg, end with rnd 8.

Shape crown
Note Change to dpns when there are too few sts to fit comfortably on circular needle.
Next (dec) rnd [K6, p2tog, p1] 16 times—128 sts.
Next (dec) rnd [K6, p2tog] 16 times—112 sts.
Next (dec) rnd [K2tog, k2, k2tog, p1] 16 times—80 sts.
Next rnd [K4, p1] 16 times.
Next (dec) rnd [K1, k2tog, k1, p1] 16 times—64 sts.

Next (dec) rnd [K1, k2tog, p1] 16 times—48 sts.
Next (dec) rnd [K2tog, p1] 16 times—32 sts.
Next (dec) rnd [K2tog] 16 times—16 sts.
Cut yarn, leaving a long tail. Thread yarn through rem sts and pull tight to close.

Finishing
With CC and tapestry needle, using photo as guide, make French knots at the center of each cable, running a continuous thread up each cable to minimize ends.
With CC, make 4"/10cm pom pom and secure to top of hat. ■

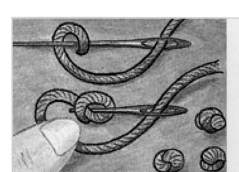

French Knots
Bring the needle up and wrap the thread once or twice around it, holding the thread taut. Reinsert the needle at the closest point to where the thread emerged.

Pom Pom Templates

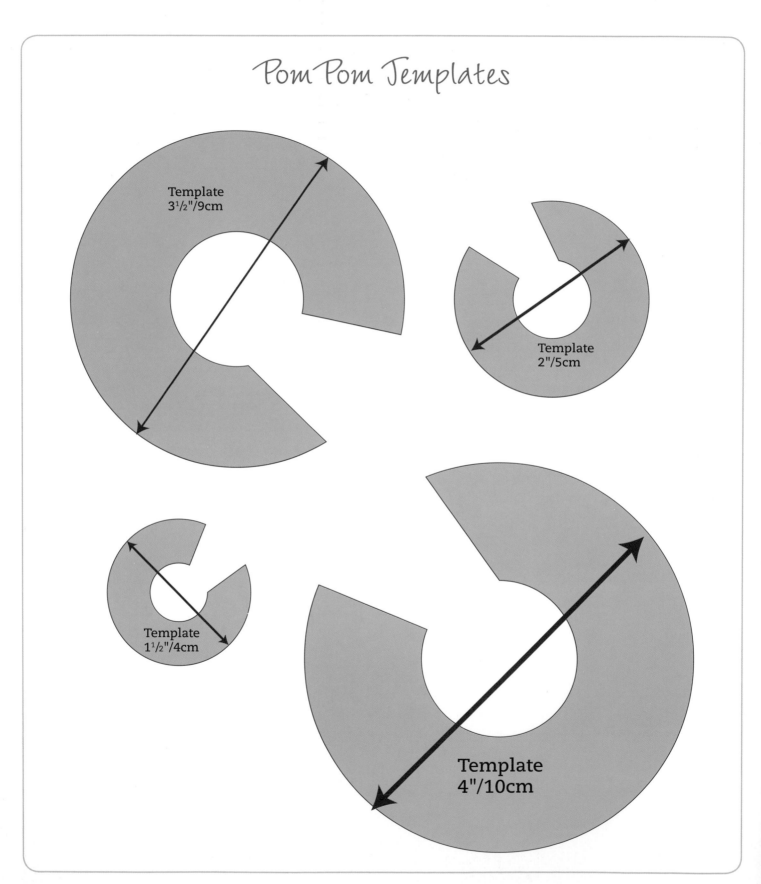

Template
$3^{1}/_{2}$"/9cm

Template
2"/5cm

Template
$1^{1}/_{2}$"/4cm

Template
4"/10cm